INDIAN TRIBES OF AMERICA

Indian Tribes
of America

by Marion E. Gridley

ILLUSTRATED BY LONE WOLF

Rand McNally & Company

CHICAGO • NEW YORK • SAN FRANCISCO

Library of Congress Cataloging in Publication Data

Gridley, Marion Eleanor, 1906–
    Indian tribes of America.

    Reprint of the ed. published by Hubbard Press,
Northbrook, Ill.
    SUMMARY: Describes the distinctive ways of life of
the major Indian tribes of the Northeast, Southeast,
Plains, and Northwest coast.
    1. Indians of North America—Juvenile literature.
(1. Indians of North America)   I. Lone Wolf,
Blackfoot Indian.   II. Title.
E77.4.G74   1976   970'.004'97   76-24843
ISBN 0-528-88581-2

Cover illustration by GEORGE ARMSTRONG

Indian tribes of many areas of the United States and Canada are
represented in the cover painting. The major figure, Sioux Chief
Red Cloud, wears a protective breastplate of bone (portrait based on
a photograph, Smithsonian Institution). The whale headdress next to
him was carved by a member of a Pacific Northwest tribe. The blower
mask, used by the Iroquois False Face Society, was made of painted
wood and human hair. Dwellers in a Zuni Pueblo in the southwestern
United States fashioned the colorful clay pot. The reed hut was
the home of a family in the Louisiana-Mississippi area.

PRINTED IN THE UNITED STATES OF AMERICA

CONTENTS

CHAPTER ONE
The Indian's World

LONG years ago people found their way to the continent of America. No one is really sure how or why they came. The accepted belief is that they came from Asia, crossing the Bering Straits and moving southward. Some say there was land between the hemispheres called Atlantis. It is said to have sunk below the ocean long ago. Believers in Atlantis say the people fled westward when it was swallowed up by the sea.

Perhaps the secret of their coming will always remain hidden in the mysteries of the past, or yet will some day come to light. It is certain that people were living in America three thousand years ago, and for ages they remained undisturbed and free to wander at will or to stay as they chose. Along the Atlantic coast and in the northeast, they were briefly visited by the sea-faring Vikings. But the Vikings did not remain long and their coming left practically no impression.

Centuries later three white-winged ships fought their way across the ocean, and the people of America received a name. Columbus, the leader of this sea caravan, thought that he had reached the land of India which he was so earnestly seeking. It was he who named these people Indians, and by that name they have been known ever since. But they had no name for themselves as a racial group—each tribe, or band, had its own individual name, and mostly the members of each band called themselves "The People." The Indian does not say that he came from any other land to this one. He says that he was always here.

America is a land of many natural features. It has three climates—cold, moderate, and warm. It has glistening desert sands, and broad level prairies, and thickly growing forests. In the east, and in the west, mountains stand in grim array. In each of these

7

different sections, the Indians lived, and the place in which they lived had its influence on the way they lived, affecting also their costumes, their music, their crafts, and their traditions.

Some were hunters and moved with the game, others were agricultural people and lived in permanent villages. In each section of the country, Nature had placed the means for men to live. Man had only to learn of and develop uses for these gifts of Nature. Whatever the place in which he lived the Indian knew the ways of Nature and how he could best turn them to his ends. By his cleverness in so doing he was able to create for himself a civilization that answered his needs and through which he progressed.

Because their lives and their customs were so influenced by the land about them, the groups living within a certain area had many customs in common, though they were different, one from the other. Because there were so many tribes, and because it is impossible to tell about them all, men of science who study people and their ways have divided the Indians according to the regions in which they dwelt. These divisions are known as the "culture divisions." So, in this book, we speak of the Woodland Indians, the Plains Indians, the Indians of the Southeast, of the Southwest, and of the North Pacific Coast.

Not all Indian tribes spoke the same language, but many spoke similar languages and these were grouped according to these similarities. Such a linguistic grouping is called a "linguistic" or "family" stock and there are about thirty of these.

Many Indian tribes were made up of clans. The clan was like a very large family, and all of its members were close relatives. The tribe was the same as a nation. Often a number of tribes banded together to form a confederacy.

In this land that he discovered, and in which he was "discovered" in turn, the Indian lived a happy and contented life, but it was far from an easy one. He could not afford to be lazy, and every man, woman, and child had to carry out his share of the labor of the village. The man was the hunter and the provider of food, the warrior and defender of the people. His work was difficult, and his duties heavy, and his life was in constant danger. When he was not actually engaged in some of these undertakings, he must be carrying on activities to keep himself physically perfect. The woman was the

8

keeper of the home. She must plant and care for the crops, gather the harvest, cook the food, tan the skins and make them into clothing.

Even the animals were better fitted to live in the wilderness country than was the Indian. They had sharp claws and horns and teeth with which to protect themselves. They had coats of fur to keep them warm when the bitter cold days set in. The Indian had to seek out and obtain from the animals his food and clothing. He had only the primitive weapons that he made himself with much labor. He might have to travel many miles in search of game and still return empty handed.

He had to develop to the fullest extent his senses of seeing and hearing, and his ability to think. The world about him was his school, and he must be the complete master of its lessons. He watched the coming and the going of the sun, the waxing and the waning of the moon. He watched the regular processions of the seasons and he knew of the habits of the birds, the fish, the animals. Every broken branch, or scratch on a rock, or imprint on the earth had a meaning, so well did he know the world in which he lived.

He was of necessity a skilled hunter, but as clever as he was, the animals also were clever. So he became ingenious in the making of traps, hooks, nets, and snares, and he developed methods to lure the animals within killing distance.

The Indian was not the wild man we are accustomed to think him. The marks of any civilization are its songs, its stories, and its arts, and the Indian had all of these. He had a rigid code of honor, and he was sincerely and deeply religious. He was not the serious, stolid person that we imagine him to be, but was happy, gay and laughing, exceedingly fond of jokes, and of playing games. He did not laugh or speak loudly before strangers, because he believed that it was most impolite to do so. The stranger might not understand his language, and on hearing laughter and raised voices, might think that he was the object of the talk or joke and be hurt or offended. With the coming of the white man, the civilization of the Indian was doomed to vanish. The killing off of the wild game left no place for the hunter. The substitution of machine made tools and implements and fabrics left no need for the products of the skilled hands of the Indian maker. Though the Indian no longer lives the old way, yet the contributions of his civilization to the betterment of the people of the world are found on every hand.

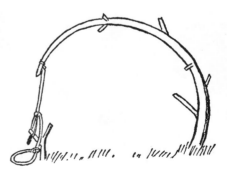

WHERE WERE
THE DWELLERS AMONG THE LEAVES?

In the northeast section of the country, from the New England states and lower Canada westward to Minnesota, and north of the Ohio River.

Some Principal Tribes of the Region	Where They Lived	Where They Are Now
DELAWARE	Delaware	Oklahoma
ERIE	Along Lake Erie	Extinct*
HURON	Between Lakes Erie and Huron	Canada, Oklahoma
ILLINIWEK	Illinois	Extinct*
IROQUOIS MOHAWK ONEIDA ONONDAGA CAYUGA SENECA TUSCARORA	New York	New York, Canada, Wisconsin, Oklahoma
KICKAPOO	Wisconsin	Oklahoma
MENOMINEE	Wisconsin	Wisconsin
MIAMI	Illinois, Indiana	Indiana, Oklahoma
MOHEGAN	Connecticut	Connecticut
NARRAGANSETT	Rhode Island	Rhode Island
OJIBWA	Michigan, Wisconsin, Minnesota	Michigan, Wisconsin, Minnesota, North Dakota, Canada
OTTAWA	Michigan	Michigan, Canada
PENOBSCOT	Maine	Maine
PEQUOT	Connecticut	Extinct*
POTAWATOMIE	Michigan, Wisconsin, Illinois	Michigan, Wisconsin, Kansas
SAUK and FOX	Wisconsin, Illinois, Iowa	Iowa, Oklahoma
SHAWNEE	Ohio	Oklahoma
SUSQUEHANNA	Pennsylvania	Extinct*
WAMPANOAG	Massachusetts	Extinct*
WINNEBAGO	Wisconsin	Wisconsin, Nebraska

*As a tribal group.

CHAPTER TWO
Dwellers Among the Leaves

Dense were the forests in our northeast country. From the Atlantic coast to the Great Lakes stretched the woods of the needled pines and dark green cedars, encrusted with brown cones. The birch was found with silver shimmering bark. Here grew the graceful elm, the sturdy ash, the pliant hickory, and the rainbow-leaved maple. Deep in the forest lay blue lakes, quiet streams, and wide rivers whose whirling rapids flecked the rocks with foam.

Here lived the Woodland Indian. The forest to him was a brother-friend, for from the forest came his store of worldly possessions—his food, his clothing, his home, and all of the things by which he carried on his mode of life. He loved the forest and he saw beauty in the climbing vines, the flowers and flower buds, and in the varied leaves. He decorated his clothing and the things that he used with designs that were inspired by these leaf and flower patterns.

To the Woodland Indian a tree was sacred and living. Every part of the tree was helpful in his struggle for existence and nearly every tree was of use. He gathered dry leaves and pith to start his fires. From the young saplings he made poles with which to build his lodge, and covered it with bark to keep out the slanting rain. He made his dishes from wood and bark, as well as his storing and some cooking utensils. His hunting implements and some of the tools with which he worked were made of wood. Tying and weaving materials came from tree and plant fibers.

In order to live the Indian had to destroy the life of the tree, and for this he was sorry. In the beginning the Great Spirit had said that the animals and the things of the forest were the helpers of man. But man must not abuse this privilege and must not

take the life of an animal or tree merely because he wished to do so. The Indian was very careful never to take more than he actually needed in order to exist. He hunted only when food was necessary, and he took from the forest only that which he required. Nothing was wasted . . . a use was found for everything.

From the trees the Woodland Indian made two of his most useful inventions; the canoe and the snowshoe. Land travel was difficult through the thickly wooded country. But the rivers led to the world beyond the horizon and the canoe made it possible to move along the waterways and lakes to distant places. Its lightness permitted one man to carry it from stream to stream, or around parts of the river that were impassable. When the snow lay drifted deep in the woods, walking was slow and exhausting. Upon his snowshoes, the hunter could follow the game with ease. Later on, these two inventions were to prove of great value to the white settler and explorer, and they are still of value today.

First, before the Indian could make use of any of this tree material, he had to know how to secure it. He did not have sharp edged tools of steel, but only the stone implements that he made himself. But he did have fire, and by the use of fire and these tools of stone, he was able to clear the land for his villages and to secure the wood that he needed. Branches were heaped around the base of a desired tree and kindled. Not far above, the trunk was girdled with clay, or wet sod, so that the flames could be controlled and the wood protected from burning. As the tree became charred from the fire, the blackened parts were hacked off with a stone axe. Gradually the flames bit through and the tree was felled.

From the young green saplings, the Woodland Indian made the framework of his home. Usually he selected the white oak for this purpose; saplings would bend without breaking. The ends were set firmly in the ground and bent over to form an arch. Where the tapering tips came together, they were wound about each other and then firmly tied with strips cut from the inner bark of the basswood. Saplings also encircled and were tied to the arched framework. Over this framework was placed the covering of overlapping sheets of birch bark, or of flattened pieces of elm bark. When the cattail rushes were tall green spears standing in the water they were gathered by the women, dried, and woven into mats. These were used for the winter covering of the house. They were waterproof and kept it snug and warm. There was also a fireplace in the center of the lodge floor and an opening in the center of the roof, so that the smoke would be drawn out of the dwelling. The covered houses looked like the rounded domes of beaver lodges. The Indians say that violent wind storms never blew them down.

In the forest there was food in plenty, providing it could be obtained. There were the large game animals, such as the deer, the bear, and the moose; and many smaller ones besides. Flocks of wild pigeons darkened the skies; there were turkeys, partridge, quail, and pheasant, and all the water birds. The rivers and lakes were plentifully stocked with fish.

For hunting weapons, the Indian had only his bow and arrows. He had a knife that he used for the cutting and skinning of game, and a stone or wooden headed club that he used as a protective and throwing weapon. But the arrow could travel faster and more silently than either of these. In the thickly wooded country a spear was of no use except for fishing.

Bows were made of second-growth hickory, of osage orange, of ash or oak. The arrows were tipped with heads of flint, or of smooth and polished antler. A turtle claw made a sharp tip, and the ankle bone of the deer formed an arrow head that would skim over the water for duck hunting. From the sturgeon came glue to fasten the feathers to the shaft. Because a boy would some day grow up to be a hunter, he had a bow as soon as he was able to handle one. But a boy's arrows were blunt-headed. They were capable of killing squirrels and small birds, and they were good learning-to-shoot arrows, for the loss of one did not matter.

Yet in spite of his bow and arrows and all of the aids that he devised to help him in his quest for food, the Woodland Indian did not rely entirely on the hunt. Results were too uncertain. He raised most of what he ate, and in his garden grew crops of corn, beans, squash, and pumpkins. These all had their origin in America before the coming of the white man.

Today, at least one-third of the products of the American vegetable garden come from the Indians, and of these, corn, perhaps is the greatest gift. No one knows the

story of how the first corn was developed except that it probably came from the wild *teocentli* grass. But it is certain that in the past four centuries the white man has made but few improvements or changes in corn and these cannot compare with the accomplishments of the Indian farmer with this plant. It was the corn of the Indian that saved the colonists from starvation. During their first hard months of life in the wilderness, it was Squanto, of Massachusetts, who taught the Pilgrims of corn and how to grow it, as well as of countless other ways to sustain themselves in the new home. The Jamestown settlement depended on the corn of the Virginia Indians. Corn was so important to the first whites that without it the peopling of America might have been delayed at least a hundred years.

Tobacco, too, was another agricultural gift of the Indian that became of great commercial worth.

Indian gardening was most simple. Digging and hoeing were done with tools of hard wood, or the shoulder blade of an animal. When the first leaves on the oak were as large as a red squirrel's foot, the Indian did his planting. Rows of small hills were made, about two feet apart. The corn kernels were planted in each hill. On the south were planted squash and pumpkins, and as these vines grew, they wound about the base of the hill and the vegetables lay upon the ground. Beans were also planted in the hill, and they clambered up the corn stalk and used it for a pole. Sunflowers stood between the corn plants. They were raised for the oil that came from their seeds. Legends told that the corn, bean and squash plants were three loving sisters that must always be planted together. But in reality, this was a most practical way to garden, and weeding was a simple matter, for only the hill itself needed to be weeded.

Besides the foods that were raised, there were the many wild things of the forest. There were all sorts of fruits, berries, and nuts. The tender leaves and buds of the milkweed or the opening fronds of ferns were the best kind of greens, though many other plants were also used for this purpose. The roots and seeds of the yellow pond lily were a special delicacy. In the spring the maple trees were tapped for the sap from which came sugar and sweet syrup.

The Woodland Indian made his clothes of deer skin, sewn with threads of sinew,

14

which is the name for dried animal tendon. He did not wear any unnecessary clothing, for in the brushy wooded country in which he lived, he had to dress for freedom of movement. Things that would catch in the tree branches or bushes would handicap him greatly. Breech cloth and moccasins were sufficient clothing during warm days. Leggings protected the limbs when traveling through the underbrush, or in cold weather. In the winter, a robe of rabbit skins, cut into strips and woven into a pliable blanket was wrapped about the body. A thick bear skin also made a good robe. Women wore dresses, leggings, and moccasins of skin, and they too had robes for winter wear. The moccasins of this region were soft soled, made of one piece of skin.

It was not easy to care for long hair in the forest country. A hunter's life sometimes depended on his ability to move swiftly, and catching hair could delay action. When on a hunt that lasted many days, or on the warpath, the Woodland Indian found it wise to shave his head but for a small piece of hair on top. This was neatly braided and was known as the scalp lock.

The scalp lock was left as an ornament, and a place for putting feathers or other articles of adornment. It was not left for the purpose of "scalp-taking" for, with the exception of a very few tribes, the Indian did not scalp until the coming of the white man. The rival governments in early American history paid bounties for the scalps of enemies, whether Indian or white, and with this encouragement, the practice of scalping soon spread rapidly.

For special occasions, a roach of dyed deer and porcupine hair was worn as a head ornament. In this roach were fastened eagle feathers that were notched or colored to indicate the deeds of bravery for which they had been earned. When the great dances were held, many young men wore these roaches. It was the skilled dancer who could, while keeping time to the drum and going through the various steps, move his head so that the eagle feather danced with him, twirling within its bone holder.

Baskets were made from the wood of the black ash or from folded pieces of birch bark. For the black ash baskets, a tree was carefully selected for straightness and freedom from knots and limbs. The bark was peeled off, and then the log was pounded until it broke into splints. These splints were stripped down so that they looked like silver rib-

bons. Then they were dyed and cut to the desired widths and woven into baskets that could be used for many years.

From the porcupine and from the moose came quills and hairs that were colored and used for beautiful embroidery work. The white man brought beads, and these soon took the place of the primitive materials and Indian beadwork became famous. Blankets were substituted for the robes of fur, and they were bordered with bits of silk cut and put together in strange yet pleasing color combinations.

In the olden days, there were more Indian tribes living within the Woodland area than in any other section of the country. From this brief description of their life it will be seen that they were farmers, and hunters, and fishermen. They were the friends and teachers of the newcomers from the Old World across the sea. It was with Woodland Indians that the first Thanksgiving feast was held, and the traditional Thanksgiving dinner is today made up of foods that were their contributions.

The early home of the Dwellers Among the Leaves is now the most important part of the United States. It has the greatest number of people living within its borders, and the largest and most important cities and centers of commerce. Many of these cities, such as Detroit and Chicago, were built upon the lodge-fire ashes of Woodland Indian villages.

PEOPLE OF THE LONG HOUSE
(The Iroquois)

In all the northeast country there were no people so powerful as the tribes that formed the Iroquois confederacy. Their villages stretched throughout the state of New York as we know it today, and they held sway over all the region about them. In their long bark houses, several families lived together—a fireplace for each family section. Sometimes a house was ten fires long.

Five tribes lived as friends and formed this ancient league of nations. Where the sun rose each morning, the brave Mohawk made their home. Where the sun set each night, the proud Seneca had their dwellings. In between were the Cayuga, the Onon-

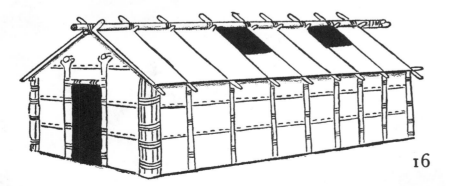

16

daga, and the Oneida. The villages ranged across the land just as the family sections were placed in the bark cabins. They thought of their land as they did of the cabins in which they lived, with each tribe a family. The home was a symbol of their land, and they called themselves the People of the Long House. The door-keepers of the west and of the east were the Seneca and the Mohawk. They were the strongest nations within the league, for they were the protectors of the others.

A long time ago these tribes did not live in harmony as brothers. Very often a red painted tomahawk, hung with scarlet feathers, was placed by silent-moving scouts before a cabin village. This was a sign that unfriendly feelings prevailed. The many wars between the Iroquois tribes were weakening and destroying their strength. They found themselves in constant danger of attack from others who lay ready to strike when they were exhausted from quarreling with one another.

There were other conditions of evil, for among the Indians, as among all people, there were those who were strong and those who were weak, and those who were neither one nor the other but something of both.

Among the Onondaga lived two men; one of these was feared and one was loved. Adodarhoh was cruel and harsh and wicked in all that he did. The Onondaga were greatly afraid of him, and because of their fear they obeyed his every wish. Hiawatha was loved by his people and he grieved for them. Many times he counseled with Adodarhoh and tried to persuade him to give up his evil ways, but he met only with bitter opposition and hatred.

Disappointed at the failure of his pleas to Adodarhoh, Hiawatha left the Onondaga and went into exile. He journeyed to the south, traveling on and on, and when he came to a new village he rested outside until the smoke from his fire was noticed and he was bidden to come within. For Hiawatha was a man of note, and it was a custom of these Indians that a famous one should not enter a village uninvited.

Wherever he went, Hiawatha heard of a great person who had come from the north to dwell among the Mohawk. The name of this person was Dekanawida. He had come among the Mohawk people paddling a canoe of white birch. Always he talked of the Great Peace and when Hiawatha heard this he was determined to find him.

Hiawatha traveled twenty-three days in search of Dekanawida, and he dreamed of the Great Peace and of what he would say to this man of the north country. When at last he stood before Dekanawida in his lodge in the village of the Mohawk, he had made plans for the welfare of his people. Dekanawida was pleased with the thoughts of Hiawatha and they became firm friends and companions. Together they worked out the Peace Plan in which the five tribes would become as one.

The plan was presented to the Mohawk who accepted it wholeheartedly. Then began Hiawatha's great work. At Dekanawida's bidding, he traveled throughout the land of the five nations. He talked of the Great Peace and strove to gain converts to its cause. From village to village and from lodge to lodge his mission led him, and he proved his statesmanship. For each tribe listened and accepted, and in the end even the wicked Adodarhoh consented to join the movement for reform.

When Hiawatha had completed his task, a council was held and the League of the Long House People was established. Together Dekanawida and Hiawatha founded the system of government and set forth its laws. Hiawatha gave to the people the gift of wampum which he had discovered on his travels and told them of the rules for its use.

Wampum was tubular beads made from shells. The wampum beads might be purple, or white, or purple and white striped. These were the natural shell colors. When other colors were desired, the beads were stained. All records of the league were kept in woven belts of wampum. The symbolic designs and the combination of colors recorded historic events. When a treaty was made and accepted, belts of wampum were exchanged with the saying: "This belt preserves our words." Wampum strings were used to send messages and in ceremonies held at the time of death. To give a name among the Iroquois was said to be "the casting of a necklace upon one's neck," for wampum strings were used to record names. The great belt of the Iroquois league had woven within it the design of an ever-growing tree. Certain men were the wampum makers, and they drilled and shaped the beads. Wampum was one of the most valuable possessions of the Iroquois and it played an important part in their rituals.

So, in this manner, the five tribal groups became united. Later on the Tuscarora were taken in as a brother-tribe, and the Long House People were then the Six Nations.

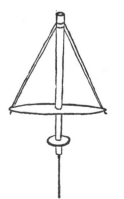

Hiawatha was not a legendary person but a real man who lived about 1459. Through his poem, Longfellow has made the name famous everywhere. But the Hiawatha of Longfellow, and the Hiawatha who was the great Indian law-giver, are two different beings.

With the forming of the league, the Iroquois villages grew in strength and number. The men were skilled hunters and famous warriors. The large garden clearings of the women were envied by all who chanced to see them. In the clearings were platforms from which the fields could be watched so that animals or birds coming to feast upon the corn could be frightened away. There were also cribs, very like ours of today, where the ears could be stored.

Corn was the staff of life to most Indians and it was cooked in many ways. It was roasted or boiled when green, or parched and pounded into meal, or made into hominy or succotash. Corn soup and corn dumplings were popular. A famous Iroquois dish was boiled corn bread. The corn was hulled, washed, and then pounded into flour. The flour was mixed with boiling water until it formed a stiff paste and then cooked beans were added. Sometimes walnuts or butternuts or one of the seasonal berries were used, but beans were preferred. When the mixing was done and the paste was kneaded until it was just the right consistency, it was formed into loaves and placed in boiling water and cooked for about an hour. When the loaves floated to the top the bread was ready.

Most unusual was the Iroquois False Face Society. Sometimes a hunter returned and told of strange experiences that had befallen him in the woods. Sometimes one dreamed at night of mysterious faces, distorted and ugly. These strange experiences were brought about by the "flying heads." The distorted faces that appeared in dreams belonged to them. The "flying heads" were spirits,—weird beings that peopled the woods. The "flying heads" were disease spirits. They were always in conflict with the Life God and he was always the victor over them, and that is why their faces were so tortured and misshapen.

When one dreamed of these mysterious faces, their power was upon him. The dreamer must carve a mask in the likeness of the face of which he dreamed, and he must wear the mask as a member of the False Face Society. When he wore the mask he lost

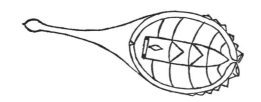

his own personality and became the one whose face he wore. The spirit of the mask was completely within him and he had the power to cure disease. If he was not treated respectfully, while wearing his mask, or if the mask was not treated respectfully, it had the power to bring about the same diseases that it could cure.

The dreamer must carve his mask upon a living basswood tree. While the face was being outlined upon the rough bark, a priest of the False Face Society chanted before it. The song that was chanted lured the "flying head" spirit. It entered the tree and found its face. The tree was then cut down but its life entered the outlined features that now had life as well as spirit. A short log bearing the face was then cut off and carried to the home of the carver. Here it was shaped into its proper form so that it could be worn as a mask. When the mask was completed a great feast was held and the ceremonies of the False Face Society took place. The feasters looked upon the new face that they might say "I know him," for it had become a friendly spirit. It was living and real and must be guarded and protected at all times. The faces were painted, some black, some red, and some white. Some faces were young, and some were old, but nearly all had deformed or twisted features.

Spring and Fall were the times for the great False Face ceremonies for these were the seasons of sickness. From house to house went the False Face dancers. They carried with them rattles made of the shells of snapping turtles. They cried aloud and made all manner of weird sounds. Even their speech was different, for in this way they frightened off evil spirits lurking about the village.

In the winter the snow snake games were held. This was an exciting game of skill and often village played against village. A log was dragged over the snow and formed a trough that was used as the runway for the snow snake. The players made their snakes of long flattened pieces of wood. One end was curved up a little. The other end was slightly notched so that the finger might have a hold for throwing. The players threw the snakes in such a way that they glided along the trough at a great speed and the side whose snakes traveled the farthest was the winner.

The Iroquois warrior was easily distinguished by his head dress, a turban shaped cap that covered a framework of splints. One splint went around the head like a band.

20

Two others formed cross arches over the head. The cap part fitted tightly over this framework and its top was covered with a cluster of white feathers. A single eagle feather arose from the midst of this white feather cluster. The chiefs wore two feathers sloping downwards. Sometimes exploit feathers were added, and these feathers were their military medals.

The Iroquois were famous for their political unity, and for their abilities in this direction. They were great statesmen and no other Indians possessed such genius for politics and organization as did they.

In their council meetings they made and carried out plans that were to affect deeply the history of America. Two of the most powerful nations of Europe—France and England—eagerly sought their friendship and often breathlessly awaited their decisions. A vast country was at stake in this race for power and firmly in the grasp of the Iroquois this prize was held. Later those who framed the American form of government drew inspiration from that of the People of the Long House—a form of government that traced back to the days of Dekanawida, the great Peace Maker, and his disciple, Hiawatha.

PEOPLE OF THE LAKES
(The Winnebago)

Red sandstone cliffs rose sharply from the waters of Green Bay. It was to this very spot that the four Thunderbirds came down from the skies. They came in a silver mist of rain and alighted upon a giant oak tree. Here they founded the Winnebago Nation. Here was the principal village called Red Banks, though Winnebago territory extended throughout central and southern Wisconsin to the Mississippi.

There were other spirit-animals that helped the Thunderbirds in the forming of this once powerful tribe. The people were separated into clans and each clan took the name of one of the spirit animals. There were twelve of these clans. Four were known as the Sky or Upper People, and eight were known as the Earth or Lower People.

Because the Thunderbird Clan was founded first, it was the most important, and

21

from this group came the tribal chiefs. A Thunderbird chief could never go on a war party for he must be the leader of his people in the ways of peace. Always he must strive to serve and help those who looked to him for guidance. Just as the Mother Bird watched over the young fledglings in her nest, so must the Thunderbird Chief watch over his people.

Every clan had its own particular duties and these duties could be carried on by no other. The Bear Clan chief was the war leader. Members of the Bear Clan enforced all of the necessary rules of hunting and warfare that prevented endangering the lives of others. Before the white man came the Bear Clan chief saw to it that no war party ever attacked a village before sunrise or after sundown. He saw to it that before an attack was made the long "halloo" of the war cry was given so that women and children might be warned to a place of safety.

If there was important news that all the village should hear about, it was the Buffalo Clansmen who were the heralds and cried the word aloud. Sometimes a council would be called by another tribe for the purpose of settling boundary difficulties, or merely for a friendly get-together. To such meetings the Waterspirit Clansmen went as the representatives of the chief. If a council fire was to be kindled, the Elk Clansmen were called, for they were the firemakers of the village.

It was an easy matter to know to what clan-family a person belonged, for from the clans the people were named. A girl might be called Floating Cloud or Walks-in-the-Rain. A boy might be known as Lightning or Big Thunder. These were Thunderbird names, because they referred to the elements, or to the sky objects. Or a boy might be called He-Who-Leaves-a-Bank-of-Yellow-Sand, or Looks Around. Such names belonged to Bear Clan members because they described habits of the bear. When the bear dug its den it banked up the earth to one side of the opening. If fearful that danger was about, it stood upon its hind legs and looked around to see if it needed to be on guard.

The Winnebago said that brothers and sisters should never quarrel, and quarrel they never did, because they never spoke to each other. While they were little children they did; they played happily together and at meal time they ate from the same bowl and used the same spoon. The carved ladle of wood was passed about the circle from one

to the other. In this way they learned to love each other and to share. Sharing was a joy and never a hardship, and the old people taught that even a kernel of corn' could be divided among several.

It was only after they became grown boys and girls that they ceased to speak to one another. A sister would do all that she could for her brother. When he returned weary from a day's hunt, she would prepare food for him. She would comb and dress his long hair and bring him fresh moccasins. She would give him cool water and perhaps sweeten it a little with maple sugar. But never did she speak to him.

A brother would protect and care for his sister always. All the man duties that were his he would perform willingly for her sake. But he would not speak to her. Where silence prevailed no harsh word could be uttered. There was never any chance for cross or unpleasant feelings to arise between brothers and sisters.

When the maple sap ran in the early spring the time was a joyous one. The swelling buds proclaimed the fact that winter was over and a new year had begun. Temporary camps were built in the maple groves, and the trees were tapped for the yearly supply of syrup. The liquid was collected in kettles made of green birch bark and hung over the fire until it thickened. It was then poured into molds of bark or wood and left to harden. A duck's bill was used as a mold to make candies for the little children.

With the fall came the wild rice harvesting. The wild rice was a principal food of the Lake People. Gathering the rice was the work of the women. Bark canoes were poled through the thickly growing plants that grew to a height of several feet. As the canoes glided along, the rice harvesters pulled the heavy laden stalks over their craft and beat them with sticks so that the rice heads fell into the bottom of the boat. When the canoe could hold no more it was paddled back to the wigwam camp where the rice was dried and made ready for hulling. Now came the man's turn to work. Great buckets were sunk in the ground, and in time to the beat of the drum, he tramped and tramped on the rice in the buckets until the hulls were worked off. The buckets were placed near a tree, or a pole, arranged so that the men could grasp it while treading the rice and not lose their balance. The rice was now placed in birch bark basins and lightly tossed about and the wind would blow away the chaff and waste material.

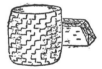

Many feasts were given during the year. Each clan gave four thanksgiving feasts so that the Winnebago celebrated forty-eight Thanksgiving Days. The clan giving the feast could not partake of the food, but there was always plenty for the others, and the people came to these gatherings in great numbers. Corn was always served at the feasts and there were many ways of cooking it.

One of the oldest methods was to roast it in the ground, and large quantities of corn were cooked in this fashion. First of all, a pit was dug about four feet wide and three feet deep. The bottom was lined with large round stones, and a fire was kept burning upon them until they were very hot. When the stones were ready the smoking ashes were cleared away and the pit was lined with corn stalks and the husks that had been stripped from the ears. The ears of corn were laid in this green bed and covered over with more stalks and husks and cold water was poured into openings that were made in the leaf blanket. Then the pit with its steaming contents was tightly packed down with earth.

All night long the corn remained in its hot resting place. The next day it was taken out. During the long hours it had cooked slowly in its own juices. It was brown and tender with a peculiar sweet flavor that is hard to describe but is delicious. It was then shelled from the ears and spread upon mats of rush and left to dry in the sun. When thoroughly dry it could be stored away for winter use and cooked as needed. The Indian cooked most of his food. Only in cases of extreme emergency would he eat raw food.

The Winnebago were expert canoe makers. The first canoe, they said, was given to them by Wakjonkaga. It was Wakjonkaga who brought many wonderful gifts to these Indians, for he was a powerful being placed in the world by the Earth Maker to be of help to His children. Wakjonkaga made the first canoe of birch bark. When it was done it floated upon the water like the warm brown leaf of an autumn oak. But Wakjonkaga was not pleased with this thing of his creation. The making of the canoe had been too easy. "This is not right," thought Wakjonkaga, "for Earth Maker has said that man must work hard for all that he has in life or he will not appreciate it. I must see that the building of a canoe is a more difficult task." Wakjonkaga broke off a bough from the hemlock tree and beat the birch until it writhed in agony from the stinging lash of the sharp needles.

24

While Wakjonkaga struck the tree, a bird sat watching. It was much distressed at the pain the tree was suffering and begged to know why it had to bear such sorrow. But Wakjonkaga only answered—"Do not ask me why. This is the will of Earth Maker and His ways are never to be questioned."

But the bird insisted on knowing why the tree must be hurt when it had given freely of its bark that a gift might be fashioned for the Indian. At last Wakjonkaga became angered. He seized the bird and threw it against the tree with all his might. Upon the trunk was left the mark of its outstretched wings and head.

"Always the imprint of your body shall be found on every birch tree," said Wakjonkaga. "Thus shall the Indian know that whomsoever displeases Him, whether it be man or bird, the Earth Maker shall punish."

The birch tree still bears upon its trunk the symbol of the One-Who-Questioned. The birch tree never grew straight again and to this day is marked with brown scars left by the hemlock switch. When the Indian made a canoe he had to piece the bark together which was hard and took much labor. A well made canoe was a prized possession and the good canoe maker was a person of importance.

With every season came a fresh round of activities that kept each person busy. The very old and the very young had work that they, too, could do to help carry on the life of the village; yet there was time for fun.

A favorite game was the Moccasin Game. This could be played anywhere, for all that was needed were four moccasins, a smooth round pebble, and a long stick. The players were divided into two sides, the "finders" and the "hiders." One member of each team was always the singer. He was a sort of cheer leader, for he encouraged the players on his side with the song, and through its words jeered and mocked the others. One player was the hider. His hands moved about, from moccasin to moccasin, always in time to the rhythm of the song and beat of the drum, and under one of the moccasins he left the pebble. The "finders" watched the "hider" very closely. Especially did they watch his hands, for sometimes the faintest twitch from a movement of the fingers would betray when the pebble left his hand and under which moccasin it lay. They would carefully study his face, for often a man would unwittingly give himself away by a smile,

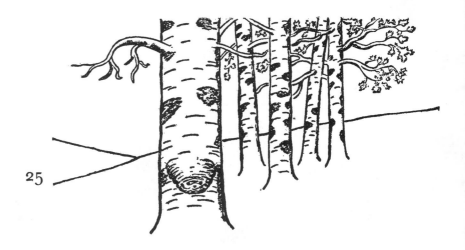

or a fleeting expression in the eyes. With the pebble hidden, one of the "finders" would then use his long stick to turn over the moccasins in his effort to locate it. There was a complicated system of scoring and a game could last many hours. Moccasin Game required skill and when really good players were on each team it was very exciting.

Most thrilling of all was Lacrosse. This was the "national game" of the tribes in the woodland area. Often one tribe was matched against another, or village against village. In playing, a ball was hurled through the air and caught in a small netted loop on the end of a stick. The player could run, holding the ball in his net, but he could never touch the ball with his hands.

Wherever the Winnebago lived there were mounds of earth. Some of these were only two or three feet high, but others were as tall as the low growing trees and very large. Sometimes the mounds were in the form of animals or birds. The Winnebago say their ancestors built the mounds and that they were used for ceremonial purposes or to signify the clan site in the village. Traditions and religious customs seemed to bear this story out. One of the most sacred and secret of Winnebago ceremonials features the building of miniature mounds.

Archeologists, too, have shared in this thought, until recently. Some of the effigy, or bird and animal mounds, have been opened and from the findings of pottery, ornaments and implements of flint, bone, shell and stone, they now believe that the mounds were made by a different people. But whether built by the Winnebago, or by other Indian groups, or by a mysterious, prehistoric race that vanished from the earth, the mounds remain as enduring records of an early civilization.

The Winnebago were great travelers, and the old people tell of journeys to the far Atlantic Coast. One of the very oldest traditions says that they watched the coming of a great canoe with shining sails while away on one of these visits. It is not clear what boat they speak of. Perhaps it was the Mayflower. It is certain that they knew the country hundreds of miles away from their home, even as far south as Florida.

Indian trails that were formed by the moccasined feet of many tribes traversing all parts of this continent were later used by the missionaries, the soldiers, and the colonists, in their march of progress.

Some of these old Indian trails that once formed a network over the entire breadth and length of our land may still be traced today. Two of the most famous are the Santa Fe Trail and the Oregon Trail. Both of these had their beginning at Independence, Missouri, but one branched off to the south and ended in New Mexico, the other continued west and northward to Willamette in Oregon. The Wilderness Road was another famous trail. It led to the west through Kentucky, Indiana, and Illinois and was well traveled by the pioneers.

Here, again, the Indian had made a contribution. He would naturally follow the shortest and most direct route, and would select his way where traveling was easiest and best. He always used the same path which was generally along high ground where there was little underbrush to slow progress. In high country, streams were few and shallow and the soil dried quickly after a rain. Trails led to trading centers, and where they ended or crossed, many of our large cities had their birth. Upon these well established trails were laid our highway routes and railroad beds, advancing the frontiers and at last spanning the continent. But the Indian hunter, trader, and adventurer first blazed the path.

27

WHERE WERE
THE DWELLERS IN THE SOUTHLAND?

In the country below the Ohio River and westward to the lower Missouri
and south to Galveston Bay.

Some Principal Tribes of the Region	Where They Lived	Where They Are Now
ALIBAMU	Alabama	Extinct*
ARKANSAS	Arkansas	Extinct*
CADDO	Louisiana	Oklahoma
CATAWBA	North Carolina	Extinct*
CHEROKEE	North Carolina	North Carolina, Oklahoma
CHICKASAW	Mississippi, Tennessee	Oklahoma
CHOCTAW	Mississippi, Alabama	Mississippi, Oklahoma
CREEK	Alabama, Georgia	Oklahoma
NATCHEZ	Louisiana, Mississippi	Extinct*
POWHATAN	Virginia	Extinct*
SEMINOLE	Florida	Florida, Oklahoma

*As a tribal group.

28

CHAPTER THREE
Dwellers in the Southland

IN the deep south there was a warm land where palm trees grew, and there was cane in abundance. This was a country of gentle rains, of fertile ground, of verdant growth. It was a country filled with game and here were the birds of brilliant color—scarlet, blue, green and yellow—the rose tinted flamingo, and the snowy-plumed heron.

Scattered throughout this region were the well fortified towns of the Indians of the lower Southeast Area. Their houses were long buildings of one or two rooms. A wooden framework was covered with interwoven cane, and over this, both inside and out, were placed woven mats. Sometimes the walls were plastered with clay that had been strengthened with cane wickerwork. Roofs were thatched with palm leaves. In the very warm section the homes were but open shelters. The houses were built to form a central square, and many of them had long open porches running the full length of the house like a veranda. High spiked logs formed a protecting wall about the village. Often the houses were built upon mounds, and there were other mounds for religious ceremonies. Mounds, too, were built as burial places. A house was for the living, for shelter and protection. A mound was for the dead—it was both a tomb and a memorial.

Before man could carve in wood, or shape a stone implement, he could pile up earth. He needed only his hands and sharp sticks for digging, and baskets for carrying the soil upon his strong back. In the building of a mound, every person could give of time and labor so that a mound was truly a symbol of the thoughts of an entire group of people. A large mound might take several years to build, but when finished it would endure through the ages.

Just as the forest Indian made great use of wood, so did these Indians make use of

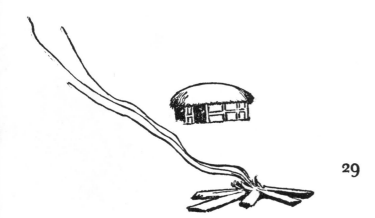

the cane that was so plentiful. It was woven into beautiful baskets and into shields and armor. It formed one of their most useful weapons—the blowgun. This was used for hunting small animals and birds. It consisted of a long cane tube from which darts of slender splints or weed stems were blown. These darts were pointed at one end. The other end was wrapped with thistle down or some such cottony substance. Blowing expelled them with considerable force and they sped through the air for a good distance. Arrows, too, were made of cane, tipped with stone, or shell, or the spurs of a turkey cock. The best bows were of the wood of the black locust.

Because these Indians lived close to the sea-coast and to the Gulf of Mexico, clams, oysters, and other shell fish formed a staple food, and the hard shells were used in many ways. One that was shaped and sharpened made a keen edged knife. Shells could be used for dishes, for ornaments, and for gardening tools.

Not much clothing was needed in the warm region. Moccasins were seldom worn except on a long journey. There was not much need for robes of fur, or garments of skin. But the people loved color and beauty, and made wonderful cloaks from the gaily tinted feathers of the birds that shared the country with them. These were worn by the warriors and great men on special occasions, and in their hair bright plumes nodded. To have the body covered with tattooing was a mark of distinction. A man could easily be a walking story book, for the cleverly drawn designs with which he was decorated told of the deeds for which he was famous.

There were many rivers and streams in the Southeast, but there was no birch for canoes. Instead, the Indian made his boat by hollowing out a tree trunk. A single log of cypress or cottonwood was roughed out with fire and finished with stone implements. Only eye-measurements were used, but the completed dugout was so carefully formed that it floated on the water with perfect balance.

The Dwellers in the Southland treasured the pearls that were found in their country. Great ropes of pearls were worn, and countless thousands of them have been found in their burial places. The Indian prized the pearls because of their loveliness. The Spaniards, coming to these shores, coveted them for their value and were ruthless in their desire to seize the lustrous gems. Even the mounds of the dead were looted, and

from one of these on the banks of the Savannah River, De Soto took some three hundred and fifty pounds of pearls.

The Indians of the Southeast were considered Woodland Indians just as were the Dwellers Among the Leaves. They, too, were farmers and hunters. They dwelt in permanent villages, and the differences in the manner of living in the north and south were slight. It was in the lower section of this southeast division that these differences were marked. Here the Indians were not so much a part of the forest as were the people to the north, for the woods were yellow pine that grew in poor and sandy soil. So the villages of these people hugged the coast line where sea-food and water fowl were plentiful, or were clustered along the river valleys where there was rich earth for farming. Such differences that existed were caused mostly by geographical and climatic conditions.

PEOPLE OF THE LIVING FIRE
(The Creek)

When the corn was ripe upon the stalks, New Year had come to the Creek Indians. With the first full moon after the corn had ripened, the ceremonies were held.

In the center of the village stood the sacred temple—the temple of the Sun. Here burned the fire that was carefully tended and never allowed to die. It was living fire, mysterious and wonderful. Only the one who was chosen for the task could tend this fire. He must guard it with his life and ever keep it burning.

But with the coming of the New Year the fire was extinguished. Houses were cleaned and repaired. Clothing was set in order and fresh garments put on. Used pottery jars were broken, baskets were discarded, and others were fashioned. There must be nothing old or worn in the village, for this was a time of newness. Even life began again, for past acts of wrong-doing were forgiven and forgotten through this ritual of moral and physical purification.

On the first day of the New Year the warriors brought four logs to the center of the village square. They were placed so that they formed a cross with their outer ends pointing to the four directions.

Eight days the ceremonies would last. There would be the singing of sacred songs and there would be many dances. There would be strange rites and the playing of games that had a special significance in this annual celebration

The fourth day was the most important of all. On the evening before, all the fires in the village were put out. The dead ashes were removed from the hearths and clean white sand was smoothed over the fireplace. At daybreak the solemn kindling of the New Fire took place.

The Fire Maker made this fire by friction. A stick known as the fire-drill was rapidly twirled between the hands or by a bow that had its string twisted about the drill. The base of this drill rested on a grooved piece of wood that had dry tinder beneath it. The spinning stick rubbed off a brown powder and created heat which soon became intense enough to cause the powder particles to smoke.

The Fire Maker now laid bits of fungus on this smouldering powder and there was a gleam of red. He then placed this glowing coal in a bunch of dried grass and faced the east for there lived the Sun, the master of fire. He swung his grass bundle from east to west and when it broke into flame it was placed in the center of the four logs and the New Fire was alight. Fire or sparks were never blown upon, for the breath contained impurities and fire was so sacred that it must always be protected from things that were profane. As the inner ends of the logs burned away they were pushed together in the center and so kept constantly burning.

When the New Fire was ablaze the Fire Maker walked about it, chanting words that none could understand. For these were the words of the Sun and so holy that it was not proper for humans to know their meaning. To the flames he offered the first fruits of the season. None could eat of the ripened corn, or of the fruits and foods of the harvest until after the ceremonies. When the offering had been made to the fire, each woman was given a share of the embers to carry to her home so that she might light her own hearth fire anew.

Creek villages were of two sorts—the "red" and the "white" towns. Before each town stood a colored pole so that it could be easily distinguished. The "red towns" were the War Towns, where blood might be shed and where lived the War Leaders. The

"white towns" were the Towns of Peace. No one could be injured in a "white town" and those who lived there must promote peace in every way. If a war council was held, the "white" townspeople must speak for peace and present every possible argument why it should prevail. White was the great "peace color." If an enemy entered the village wearing white feathers and with white painted mouth, none might lift a hand against him. He was under the protection of the Peace Town and could dwell there unharmed.

The Creek were fond of all sorts of running games, and ball games. Their athletes were regularly and carefully trained for playing, for the sports were strenuous and required physical perfection. A favorite game was that of the stone disk, called Chunkey. Chunkey yards were a part of every village. The stone disk was rolled along the ground and the player slid after it a long stick that was curved at one end. The purpose was to throw the stick in such a way that when the disk toppled to the ground it would rest within the curved crook.

Coontie was a favorite food of these people. Coontie was made from the roots of a native plant, ground and pounded into a flour and baked into cakes. A sort of bread was made from the dried fruit of the persimmon, and a part of the palm furnished a food that tasted like cabbage.

Where the Creek lived there were many streams, and along these waterways the Indian towns and fields were located. Because of this, they became known as the Creek People. In their life and customs they had much in common with the ancient civilizations of old Mexico. Their traditions told of having migrated from a land far to the west. The temples, the houses built around a central square, and the ever-burning fire, were crude representations of the complex and wonderful Mayan and Aztec civilizations. These could well indicate a connection in some remote past.

WHERE WERE
THE DWELLERS ON THE PLAINS?

The Plains Area covered a large territory, bounded on the west by the Rocky Mountains, beginning at the Mackenzie River in Canada and running south to the Rio Grande. The eastern borders were in about the center of our present states of the Dakotas, Nebraska, Kansas, Oklahoma, and Texas. The eastern parts of Montana, Colorado, and Wyoming were within the Plains country.

Some of the Principal Tribes of the Region	*Where They Lived*	*Where They Are Now*
ARAPAHO	Wyoming, Colorado	Wyoming, Oklahoma
ARIKARA	North Dakota	North Dakota
ASSINIBOINE	Montana	Montana, Canada
BLACKFOOT	Montana, Canada	Montana, Canada
CHEYENNE	Colorado	Oklahoma, Montana
COMANCHE	Texas	Oklahoma
CROW	Montana	Montana
GROS VENTRE	Lower Canada	Montana
IOWA	Iowa	Kansas, Oklahoma
KANSAS	Kansas	Oklahoma
KIOWA	Texas	Oklahoma
MANDAN	North Dakota	North Dakota
OMAHA	Nebraska	Nebraska
OSAGE	Missouri	Oklahoma
OTO	Nebraska	Oklahoma
PAWNEE	Nebraska	Oklahoma
PONCA	Nebraska	Oklahoma
SIOUX (Dakota)	Dakotas	Dakotas, Nebraska
WICHITA	Oklahoma, Texas	Oklahoma

CHAPTER FOUR
Dwellers on the Plains

BETWEEN the frontiers of the forest and the grim, towering mountains lay broad rolling country. It stretched to the far horizon, open for miles in every direction.

In this country there were few of the friendly trees that were so helpful to the Woodland Indians. There was no cane that was so useful to the Dwellers in the South. But there was the buffalo, and from this great animal the Plains Indian obtained all that he needed in order to live. His thoughts, his ceremonies, his songs and stories often centered about this mighty creature. From the buffalo skin came clothing, lodge covering, cooking utensils, and material for boats. Its flesh was food. Its horns and bones made weapon points and tools, implements and glue, and from the hair came yarn for weaving. Where the buffalo traveled there must go the Plains Indian for he depended on the buffalo for his very existence.

When these Indians first wandered onto the plains and settled in that country they lived in round earth lodges. For the greater part of the year they roamed the prairies, hunting game and living in small conical tents of skin. But always they returned in the Fall to their earth lodge villages where the older people, the women, and children had remained to care for the gardens.

Then into the southwest came the Spaniards, bringing with them herds of spirited horses. Some of these escaped and found their way to the wide plains. Wandering horse met wandering Indian and became to him "Shunka-Wakan," or "mystery dog." With the coming of the horse the Plains Indians entered their Golden Age. Miles could be traveled in a single day on horseback, and the game could be followed with greater ease. Before they had to go slowly and on foot. The horse changed their entire mode of life and

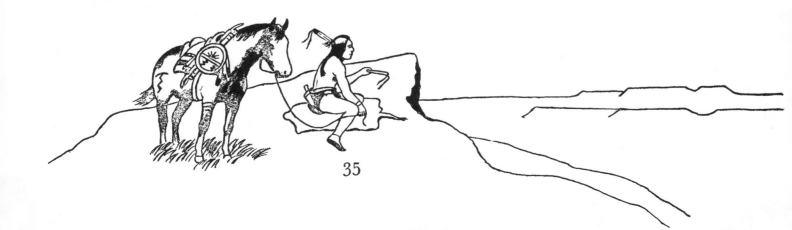

35

they became true nomads. They gave up their earth lodges and their gardens, and used only the skin house, for in moving about from place to place they needed a home that could move with them. In the early days of foot-travel dogs were used to transport the small shelters then used. But a horse could carry heavier burdens and so the lodge became a good sized dwelling. With the fleetness of the deer and the freedom of the wind the Plains Indians rode across the prairies. Each day brought new adventures and new scenes. If they wished, they could go on long trading journeys. Or they could swoop down upon another tribe and run off the grazing horses that their own herds might be increased. Plains groups have been known to travel two thousand miles.

Before the coming of the horse the buffalo herds were stampeded over the edge of a cliff and were killed by the fall. But mounted on their swift steeds, the hunters could race alongside the fleeing animals and with their bows shoot them down at a gallop. The Indians became expert horsemen, and the horse became a symbol of wealth. Horses and buffalo robes were the trade goods of the region.

A wandering life demanded a house that was not a great deal of trouble, and for such a life the tipi of the Plains could not be improved upon. It had to be a light house— one that could be easily put up or taken down, for the women did much of this work. If an enemy were advancing to attack, the men must spend all their energies getting ready for battle. Should the buffalo herds suddenly begin to move, the village must make ready to follow. Scouts were always watching these herds, and when it was necessary for the village to break up there were many tasks that required the attention of the men.

A tipi consisted only of a few poles, some stakes, the hide covering, and wooden pins to fasten this covering to the frame. Two women could put one up within half an hour. In the summer the tipi was cool and airy, for the sides could be raised to let the breeze blow through the dwelling. In the winter an inner lining kept out the cold and damp. Wind did not blow the tipi over for the stakes held the covering to the ground. At the top two flaps or ears were held upright from the smoke-hole by poles, and could be set in accordance with the direction of the wind. They controlled the draft so that the smoke from the central fireplace was blown out of the lodge. In stormy weather these flaps could be adjusted to close the opening and keep out rain or snow.

Tipi poles were made of lodge-pole pine, of spruce, or cedar. The Indian of the Plains could not use the flexible saplings of the Woodland Indian. His poles had to be straight slim trees that would stand erect with strength. He might have to travel many miles to find the wood for poles; they were highly prized and used as long as possible.

The winds usually swept across this wide expanse of country from the west, and so the tipis faced the east with most of the poles in the framework sloping so that they could brace against the pressure of the wind. The finished tipi was beautiful in appearance, of graceful and imposing line. Designs that had a symbolical meaning were painted on the outside. A tipi camp was always circular in form. The circle was a sacred figure, for the circle was protection. The sun that gave light and life and warmth was round in form. Even the earth was round and above the earth was the great circle of the sky.

When the tribe was on the move, the tipi was no longer a house, but a means of transportation. The tipi poles were formed into a V-shaped frame, secured to a rawhide harness, and fastened to a pony as if he stood between shafts. The free ends dragged upon the ground, and the household effects were carried on these dragging poles. This arrangement was called a travois.

The Plains Indian could not be bothered with things that were cumbersome or awkward to carry. Everything that he used was easy to transport. He did not make any pottery or basketry, but instead he used light, stiff rawhide, from which he made large envelopes and boxes for carrying belongings and for storage purposes. These rawhide cases, or parfleches, were painted in various patterns of diamond-shaped figures of brilliant and contrasting coloring. Plains Indian designs were always squares, or diamonds, or triangles. Rawhide was also used for moccasin soles.

Round willow frames, like great bowls, were covered with buffalo hide, and this was the boat of the region. Even this boat could be carried upon the travois. The rivers were the highways of the Indian of the woods, but the buffalo trail was the road of the Indian of the plains. Where there was a river it had only to be crossed, and these tubs of hide, called "bull boats," were needed merely to ferry heavy loads when a river barred the way.

Meat was the principal article of food. Some few tribes practiced agriculture, but

37

nearly all vegetable food was wild. Wild cherries and red willow berries, the wild potato and wild onion, and the roots of the camas were eagerly sought. Fish abounded in the streams and rivers but the true Plainsman scorned to touch them.

The shield of the Plains Indian was his most sacred possession. It was especially adapted for this open country where there was very little timber or underbrush. The spear, or lance, was also carried in warfare. No warrior might carry a shield until he had first received permission to do so through some bird or animal that came to him in a dream. The dream spirit would tell him how many shields he might make, and how they must be painted and decorated. He would also tell the warrior how he might paint and decorate himself and his pony, and these markings could never be used by any other member of the tribe.

The Plains warrior was a picturesque figure. His skin clothing was fringed and banded with strips of colored porcupine quill embroidery. His long black hair hung in braids over his shoulders or flowed loosely down his back. The beautiful wide-spreading feather war bonnet added to his dignity of bearing.

The finest bonnets were made from the white, black-tipped tail feathers of the "war" eagle. There was no other bird so majestic, or so solitary. Its home was on the high crags and it soared to lofty heights where no other bird could go. It was strong and fierce, and mysterious. It ruled the skies and the shadow of its flight could be seen upon the prairie. To catch an eagle was one of the most difficult and dangerous feats of hunting. No wonder that the price of one perfect tail of twelve feathers was a good pony. The eagle feather crown was the mark of the great warrior. Every feather had to be earned and some men might live a whole lifetime and earn only one or two feathers. Not even a chief would wear an eagle feather unless he had won the right to do so through deeds of bravery.

There were a number of these different war honors, and the way the feathers were worn or marked, told of how they had been achieved. The highest honor of all was to strike an enemy in the midst of battle—to touch him with the hand or a light wand known as the "coup-stick," for this was far more dangerous than to kill. If the "coup" was counted while charging on horseback the feather might be tipped with red-dyed

horse hair. The feather bonnet could only be worn after at least ten war honors had been earned, and even then the record must be exceptional and outstanding.

The bonnet was highly symbolical, for the circle of feathers stood for the council ring of warriors. The crown inside this feather circle was covered with eagle down and from the center of this down rose the guide, or great exploit feather. This was a long quill with a fluffy tip and it symbolized the owner of the bonnet. It took many days to make such a headdress, for the event was always marked by feasts and ceremonies. The story of each feather had to be told before it was placed with the others. If the deed that won the feather was not witnessed by any of the other braves, absolute proof as to the rightfulness of the claim had to be presented.

This free open country that permitted the wearing of the feather bonnet, also permitted the use of long distance signals. Any movement or object on the prairie could be seen afar. And so, with smoke, or fire, or by the movements of men on foot or horseback, the Plains Indian found a way to send his thoughts across the miles. Smoke was used by day and it was the signal most quickly observed, for scouts were always on the watch and certain high places were known to be signal stations. At this sending place a fire was built and over the smouldering wood the signaler placed his blanket and then withdrew it so that a round smoke cloud ascended into the sky. With these puffs of smoke—their number, or the slowness or fastness with which they were sent—the story was relayed of the discovery of an enemy or of game, and appeals were sent to flee for safety, or to hurry to attack. Fire signals were used at night.

One of the motion signals was to ride or run in a circle; this signified a discovery. A keen-eyed scout could easily distinguish such action from any direction. If the signaler held his blanket in outstretched arms and dropped it slowly to the ground, his message was that he had spied a herd of buffalo. If he rode rapidly back and forth in seeming confusion, and waved his blanket above his head, he told bad news of the sighting of a foe. When the white trader came into the Plains country he brought mirrors with him. The Indian quickly made use of the wonder-glass for the sending of signals. Flashing streaks of light caught from the sun were read just as were the puffs of smoke or the glare of flame in the darkness.

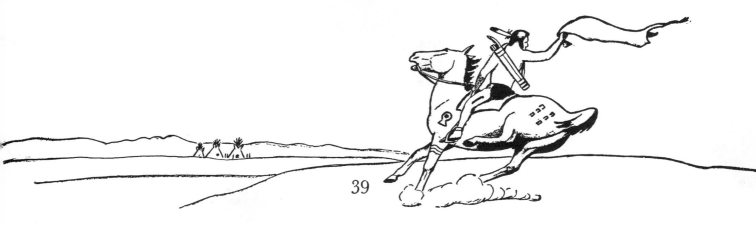

There was even a system of hand signals or sign talk. Every Indian tribe spoke a different tongue. The Plains groups speaking many different languages frequently met. By using hand signals or signs they could hold long conversations of great detail though they could not understand each other's words. Just as the circle riding meant to "Stand by, a message is coming," the waving of the hand back and forth meant that talking was about to begin, or that a question was to be asked. The Sign Talk was graceful and beautiful in use. It is said to be the best gesture language ever invented by any race of people, for the meanings of the signs are clever and understandable. Though this was a language by which stranger groups could meet and talk in friendship, it was also of great value on the warpath. A warrior could send word to another without using his voice and by the sound betraying his presence. For use in the dark there was a language of handclasps and grips, body tappings and finger tracings.

The killing off of the buffalo herds doomed the way of life of the Indian hunter of the Plains. He could not follow his nomad existence without the great animal around which his whole civilization had been built. Because of the romance of his way of life, his courage and bravery that won him respect as a warrior, the beauty and impressiveness of his feather headdress, and the sadness of his story, the Plains Indian has made the most striking appeal to the imagination. Together the buffalo and the Indian passed from the western scene and in their passing became symbolical figures—the one typified America, the other typified its Indian people.

PEOPLE OF THE SKIN LODGES
(The Blackfoot)

Crisscrossing the prairie were the wide travois trails of the Blackfoot. They knew the mountains that were purple shadows on the distant line of the sky. They had traveled far to the west to the shores of the great water that was heavy with salt. Even the warm land of the south had been visited but the Blackfoot preferred their own country of grassy plains and painted buttes.

With the rising of the sun the Blackfoot village came to life. The women were busy

building up the fires, preparing the morning meal, and carrying wood and water. The lodges were always pitched close to a stream and with the break of day the men and children walked down to the river bank and plunged in. Winter and summer, in stormy or pleasant weather, this was a daily ritual, for they believed that it made them strong and healthy and helped them to endure the bitter cold during the winter hunts on the prairie. It was a rule of an Indian camp that drinking water must be taken from a point upstream. Below this the men might bathe, and still farther below, the women. Through this sanitary precaution, the drinking water was protected from contamination.

If the camp was to be moved, the men and boys rounded up the large herd of horses and the women took down the lodges, packed the possessions and loaded them upon the travois or upon the pack animals. The chiefs and the band of Braves, or Soldiers, rode in advance of the column of marching women, children, dogs and horses. Far ahead were the scouts searching for signs of game or of enemies. Ranging on each side were the warriors, heavily armed and ready to protect the advancing column from attack or danger.

When the Blackfoot traveled they carried their fire along with them. A buffalo horn was lined with moist, rotten wood, and slung over the shoulder by a thong. The open end of the horn was fitted with a wooden stopper. With the signal to march, the carrier of the fire-horn took a live coal from the one remaining fire and put it in the fire-horn. He then carefully extinguished the last campfire. Indians knew the cruelty of fire too well to leave any embers, for the flame that warmed a lodge could also burn it down.

On top of the coal within his horn, the fire bearer placed a piece of punk that came from a fungus growth found on birch trees. The horn was then tightly closed, and the punk smouldered within its air tight chamber. When needed, new punk was added. The first young men who reached the appointed camp ground gathered brush and wood and formed piles in three different places. As soon as the fire-horn carrier arrived he hastened to one of the piles, turned out his glowing punk and tended it until the fire was lighted. The other wood piles were kindled from this one. When the women arrived and the lodges were set up, they started their own cooking fires from the coals of the three that were lighted first.

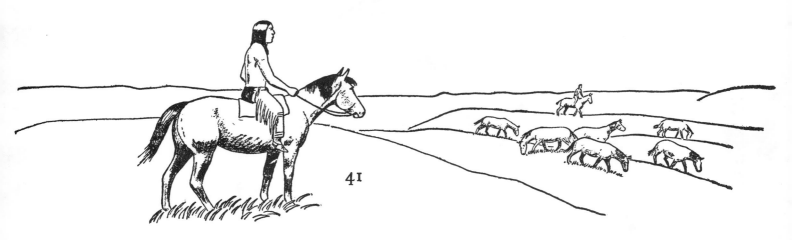

41

The day was always crowded with interest and activity. For the women there would be the tanning of skins, the drying of meat, the making of pemmican. Pemmican was a food made of pounded dried meat, dried berries or fruit, and buffalo fat. It could be eaten cold, and was very nourishing. Hunters and scouts could carry small amounts of pemmican with them and travel without fear of hunger.

A man's day would be filled with hunting, feasting, dances and games. A much-played game of the warriors was that of "Hide the Bone." Two small oblong bones were used, and one of these was marked with a black ring. The players were divided into two sides, and the singer began his weird chant that started like a gentle sound in the distance. It increased in tone until it reached a high pitch, when it sank quickly to deep low sounds, and so rose and fell continuously throughout the game. In perfect time to this song, and with graceful and intricate swayings and movements, a player skillfully changed the bones from one hand to the other. This was a confusing attempt to make it impossible for the one opposite him to guess in which hand the black marked bone was concealed.

Certain men of the tribe were the killers of eagles. The man who set out on this most dangerous task selected a place on top of a butte and here he dug a pit in the ground for a hiding place. Earth removed from the hole was carried away or scattered about, for the eagle was a wary bird with a sharp eye for any suspicious signs. Long before daylight the hunter crawled within his pit and roofed it over with small willow sticks and scattered grass, some earth and stones so that its appearance would be no different from the surroundings. On top of this covering a piece of meat was laid. A rope was fastened to the bait and firmly held by the hunter in the pit. There was nothing to do now but to wait patiently until morning when a flying eagle would spy the meat and swoop down upon it. Finding that it could not carry the meat away it would pause to feed. The eagle catcher would reach through a crevice in the pit covering and catch the eagle by the legs, dragging it into the pit and killing it. The eagle was a fierce fighting bird with cruel, sharp talons. The great white-headed eagle was so powerful that it could kill a person if angered.

The Blackfoot, like other Dwellers on the Plains, liked to paint their tipis with

42

symbolic designs and pictures. Blackfoot tipis were easily recognized for they were characterized by a dark band of color at the top and at the bottom. The band at the top represented the sky and evenly spaced upon it were round spots that were meant to be the stars. The lower band signified the earth and this, too, was spotted. These circles stood for a mushroom-like growth that the Blackfoot called "star-dust." The Blackfoot were one of the strongest of the Plains groups. It is said that during a time of warfare they crossed over a burned prairie and stained their moccasin soles black, from this event receiving their name.

PEOPLE OF THE EARTH LODGES
(The Pawnee)

From the beginning of their knowledge, the Pawnee had lived in homes of earth. Their dwellings were dome shaped, about forty feet in diameter and fifteen feet high. The earth was laid over a framework of poles and the roof was supported by stout posts. The entrance-way was an earth covered passage and every lodge faced the east.

The earth lodge was a large and comfortable house. The dome shaped roof was much used as a place to sit and talk or rest, or from which to watch the activities of the village. But more than this, the earth lodge to a Pawnee was full of meaning. It told the story of their creation, for the round floor symbolized the earth circle, the dome of the roof the sky arch, and the supporting posts the stars. The Pawnee believed that they were descended from the stars and when they had come upon the earth they were placed in earth-lodge villages, each with a star guardian. The villages were located in positions relative to each other and similar to the relative positions their star guardians held in the heavens. Each village had been given a sacred bundle that contained articles symbolical of these heavenly beings and these bundles were the great religious objects of the tribe.

The Pawnee loved the stars and there was no ceremony that did not have some connection with them. In their Hako prayer for peace the painting of a white ear of corn with blue tip symbolized the sky dwelling place. This was the most sacred part of the ritual.

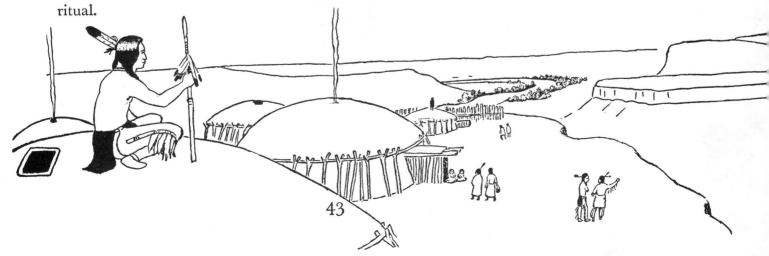

43

The Pawnee remained in their homes of earth and did not become true wanderers as did the other Plains groups. Though they were skillful hunters and roamed the prairies far and wide during the seasons of the buffalo chase, they were also tillers of the soil. Between the time of planting in the spring and the fall harvest, they left their homes in the care of those not strong enough or too young to take part in the hunt for necessary meat and skins. In the winter the buffalo hair grew long and thick, and the Pawnee hunted again. For in the cold months, the skins were at their finest for making robes.

But, though they hunted the buffalo and made use of its flesh and its hide, it was never as important to them as the corn. For corn had been given to the people when they first came upon the earth. Corn grew from the earth and because it fed and nourished man it was the symbol of all womanhood. Only a woman might plant and care for the corn for it was woman's task to nourish man and give him food. Only a man could use the bow and arrow. The bow and arrow was the symbol of all mankind, for it was the protector of the village. It was a man's task to guard and protect his people always.

Of all the people of the Plains, the Pawnee were looked upon as the most cunning of scouts. So skillfully could their young men imitate the wolves that slunk across the prairies, that they were rarely detected by night or by day. Wolves were common in the olden days and at night they ventured close to the Indian villages and often dared to walk among the lodges. So clever were the Pawnee scouts in their wolf-pretending, that they were able to draw near to an enemy village and thus observe the general lay-out.

A Pawnee warrior never traveled without the wolf skin which he used for his animal disguise. With the skin thrown over him, and moving upon his hands and knees, he trotted about in such accurate imitation that he was not suspected. In country where it was necessary to go with caution it was often important that a scout take careful observations from a high elevation. A man walking to the top of a hill could be seen and recognized from a long distance away. But a man running up a hill on his hands and knees, with a wolf robe thrown over him, would look like a wolf from the distance. He could then sit down upon the hilltop and scan the country at his leisure, for no one would look a second time at a wolf sitting upon his haunches and sniffing the air!

A Pawnee hunter also put this art of imitation to good use. Under his wolf skin, he

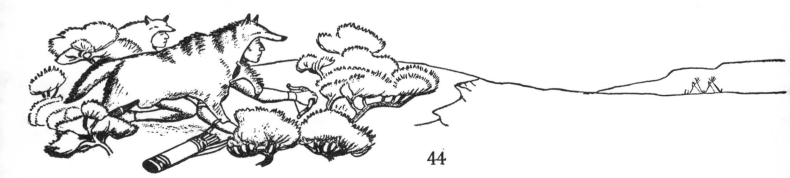

could crawl up close to the buffalo herds and shoot the animals down with the bow he carried. The buffalo did not see well. The crawling figures looked like wolves, and the buffalo were so accustomed to the gray animals that followed the herds that they saw nothing unusual. The practice of the wolf-disguise was not solely used by the Pawnee but they were considered the most crafty in employing it.

Just as did all Indians, the Pawnee found pleasure in games that developed them physically, or that developed their senses to the highest degree of usefulness. A popular game was played with arrows. The leader shot an arrow so that it fell upon the ground about sixty paces from where he stood. The players then tried to shoot their arrows to fall directly across the first arrow. All arrows shot during the play were the reward of the one who accomplished this feat, or were divided if several were successful.

It is believed that the name, Pawnee, means "horn," and that it refers to the custom among the men of dressing the hair so that it stood nearly erect and curved backward with the appearance of a horn. In the picture drawings that were the only form of Indian writing, the drawing of a horn stood for a Pawnee. But in the sign language, the gesture that described the Pawnee also described the wolf, and no doubt referred to their custom of disguise that won for their scouts respect and envy.

A ceremonial headdress of the Pawnee was made of the skin of the otter. It was wrapped about the head in turban form with the tail stiffened and projecting from the side like a long wing. Two eagle feathers stood erect at the back. The feather on the right was the taller of the two. It was decorated with a band of finely woven colored horse hair and a colored tuft. The feather on the left was plain and without decoration. These feathers stood for man and woman.

The eagle was the bird of Tirawa, who was the god of the Pawnee. The shaded feathers of the eagle—half dark and half light—told of Tirawa's plan of the universe. All things in the world are in two. Everything that lives or grows must be in two, Tirawa had said, for only in this way could life continue.

The Pawnee believed that as the feathers on the eagle were blended in color, so Life was blended. In Life there is good and evil, joy and sorrow. In Life there is weakness and strength, ugliness and beauty, and each must perfectly balance the other.

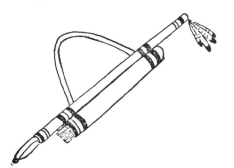

45

WHERE WERE

THE DESERT PEOPLE?

The southwest country of Texas, Arizona, New Mexico, southern California,
Nevada and Utah.

Some Principal Tribes of the Region	Where They Lived	Where They Are Now
APACHE	Arizona, New Mexico	Arizona, New Mexico
NAVAJO	Arizona, New Mexico	Arizona, New Mexico
PAPAGO	Arizona	Arizona
PIMA	Arizona	Arizona
PUEBLOS	Arizona, New Mexico	Arizona, New Mexico

    ACOMA
    COCHITI
    HOPI (12 towns)
    ISLETA
    JEMEZ
    LAGUNA
    NAMBE
    PICURIS
    POJOAQUE
    SANDIA
    SAN FELIPE
    SAN ILDEFONSO
    SAN JUAN
    SANTA ANA
    SANTA CLARA
    SANTO DOMINGO
    TAOS
    TESUQUE
    ZIA
    ZUNI

UTE	Utah, Colorado	Utah, Colorado

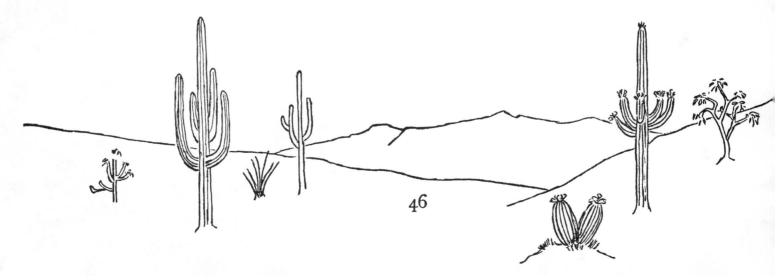

46

CHAPTER FIVE
Dwellers on the Desert

IN the far southwest lay the land of little rain. The mountain ridges of the Rockies reached down into the country like the fingers of a giant hand, and between these fingers the desert lay warmed by the sun. Ages before, great rivers had wound their way across this land, and had carved out deep canyons and high tablelands called mesas. But the passing years brought many changes and most of the rivers disappeared. Only the canyon walls remained to tell of their existence.

The ragged mountain peaks are crowned with snow. During the warmest season this snow melts and finds its way down the mountain side to bring to the few remaining rivers their little water supply. Along the river banks grow the cottonwoods, the sycamores, and willows, and on the desert itself are the spiny cactus and the sharp leaved yucca. But this is not a land of trees and plants.

The desert world is a world of color. The layered rock walls of the canyons are deep-tinged red and violet striped with tones of yellow. When bathed in the bright rays of the sun they gleam with all the colors of the rainbow. The sky is clear and brilliant blue, the earth a shimmering level of golden sand. Even the ears of corn are colored— blue or lilac, rose or burnished red, amber, white, or dusky black.

The Indians who came here were home builders. From poles and willow twigs they made rude shelters, plastered over with desert mud. They learned to make baskets from the plants and grasses and they cooked in these baskets that were so tightly woven they would hold water. Hot stones were dropped into them with crude tongs, and the water was thus heated and brought to a boil.

In this difficult country of heat and dryness, of sweeping winds and swirling sand

47

storms, the people lived and prospered. Their gardens flourished and in time they began to make pottery. Pottery bowls were good for storing water and they were better vessels in which to cook than the basket ones.

Then from the north came a wilder group of Indians. They stormed the villages and destroyed and plundered the gardens. The newcomers drove the settled ones up to the high cliffs where they defended themselves by hurling down stones and rocks upon their attackers.

Homes were built anew in the natural caves of these steep cliffs, for the desert was no longer a safe place in which to live. Walls of stone plastered with clay or adobe partitioned the living quarters. There were whole villages of these stone rooms tucked away in the cliff crevices. High towers were also built from which the countryside could be watched for signs of raiders. The cliff dwellers still cared for their gardens upon the desert floor. They worked in them during the day and returned to their cave homes at nightfall.

Desert gardens were well tended. Some of the Indian people learned to keep them always watered by means of ditches that directed the flow from the river. A ditch might be many miles long and three or four feet deep, and was well plastered with clay. Smaller ditches formed a network over the fields and connected with the main one and water could be sent to all sections of the field when needed.

In some places it was not possible to carry out this method of watering the fields, or irrigation. Then the seeds were planted deeply in the ground, and very early. In low parts of the desert the soil is slightly moist about eight inches below the surface. Seeds were planted deep enough to reach this moist soil that was not sufficiently damp to cause them to sprout. For weeks the seeds would lie in the warm ground, but when the rainy season began they would grow very rapidly. The seeds were placed quite far apart and small wind-breaks of twigs and branches were made about the plants so that the desert winds would not blow away the top sand and lay the roots bare. Plant scientists of today are now putting into practice this method that the desert Indians have used for generations. Corn seeds that have been kept in a warm, dark room with very little moisture seem to grow much more rapidly after planting.

For a long time the Indians remained in their stone villages. Notched logs were placed against the cliff edges and the people used these as ladders. They had to have their hands free for climbing and so they carried their burdens carefully balanced on their heads. Water was carried up to the houses in pottery bowls. Food was carried up in baskets.

Many years later the people left their cliff towns and settled again in the valleys, or on the mesa tops. But they still carried on many of the customs of their high, rocky homes.

In this country where rain was so infrequent and so important it became the all absorbing interest in the lives of the people. Their dances and ceremonies were prayers for rain, and their designs and symbols spoke of things that had to do with this life-giving element. Terraced edges upon a bowl pictured the high banked clouds that massed before the coming of the silver downfall. Jagged lines of lightning reminded of the storms. Growing corn figures spoke of the need for rain that the plants might live and crops be plentiful.

A wild cotton grew upon the desert and the Indians wove this into kilts and blankets and cloth for garments. Moccasins were really boots that shielded the legs from the prickly plants and cutting pointed rocks. Robes were woven from feathers of the turkey. The wild turkey had been domesticated and children cared for the village flocks.

Influenced by the painted land about him, the desert dweller loved color. Most prized of his possessions was the turquoise, the blue stone that seemed fallen from the sky. A man was poor indeed who did not have a bit of this lovely stone. It was ground into beads and cut into pendants and formed into mosaics. All the people wore turquoise and it was also used for ceremonial offerings. With those who dwelt much further to the south, turquoise was traded for the gaily tinted feathers of parrot and humming bird, and for color-changing shells. Turquoise was a gift of the gods, and when the sky was clear tradition said that the Bearer of the Sun rode forth upon a turquoise colored horse. In one of the ancient cliff dwellings, thirty thousand of the blue beads were found in a single room.

In old Mexico, the Spaniards heard tales of a people that lived to the north and that were rich with gold and silver and precious stones. Searching for these people of untold

wealth, they found only the simple Indian villages with their houses of stone or adobe. Each village might have several hundred of these houses and a thousand or more Indian inhabitants.

To these villages the Spaniards gave the name of "pueblos," which meant "town." The people became known as the Pueblo Indians, and though they are made up of a number of different tribes, the name given by the Spanish has long been used for all the town dwellers of the Southwest.

PEOPLE OF THE MESAS
(The Hopi)

Perched on the high table lands were the terraced stone and plaster houses of the Hopi. House stood upon house—the roof of one was the front yard of the next. Ladders reached from roof below to house above and these were the stairways. In times of danger the ladders could be drawn up and the house was an isolated fort. This was the type of dwelling in which all Pueblo folk lived—they had the first apartment houses in America.

Far below the mesas stretched the fields of corn, beans, squash and peppers. These gardens might be many miles away, and the men would run back and forth every day in order to care for them. Among the Hopi the man was the gardener, and this constant running and climbing developed a marvelous ability to go far on foot. Hopi men were accomplished long distance racers.

Gardens had to be protected from the great numbers of rabbits that ate the tender leaves of the young plants. Each man carried a long flat stick, slightly curved, so that when thrown it would twirl through the air. When a long-eared furry body dashed from underfoot, the stick was hurled in such a way as to hit the rabbit upon the head. Rabbit skins could be made into light, warm robes, and rabbits were good to eat. Sometimes the whole village of men and boys went out on an organized rabbit hunt, and this became an exciting contest.

The women were the basket and pottery makers. The women ground into flour the corn that was raised by the men. A large sloping stone with rough uneven surface was

50

used, and the corn kernels were rubbed against this with a smaller stone. The fine meal was mixed with water and baked in tissue-thin cakes upon a hot stone griddle. This bread was called piki, and the Hopi were very fond of it.

As the women crushed the corn kernels they would sing, grinding in perfect time to the rhythm of the song. Every so often this rhythm would change. Then the movements of the arms would change so that tired muscles could be rested, without interrupting the work. The Hopi loved to sing, and nearly every act of their daily life was accompanied by song. Even their speech was musical, and the Hopi said that it had been taught to them by the mocking bird.

In every village there was a sacred underground chamber called the kiva. The Hopi believed that they had once lived in an underworld home, far below the surface of the earth. The kiva was symbolical of that early home, and there was always an opening in its floor for others who might some day wish to come forth on to the land.

Long years in the past, the people said, there lived among them the Rain Maker gods. They danced within the village plazas and brought the precious drops of water. These gods were called Katchinas. But as time went on, the Katchinas came no more. To bring the rain, the Hopi had to pretend that they were these friendly spirits. They had to dress like them, wear masks to represent their faces, and dance and sing for rain just as the Katchinas did ages before. When a man placed a Katchina mask upon his head, he was no longer a man. He was really the life-bringing rain god.

The face of a Katchina was too holy to be looked upon by a mortal and its face was masked by clouds. So it was that one who took the place of a Katchina must always wear a mask during the ceremonies. There were many kinds of Katchinas and so there were many different kinds of masks. All were brightly colored and painted, with designs of clouds and rain, thunder and lightning, or the rainbow. The masks covered the heads completely and son.e had towering ornaments. Small dolls were carved from cotton-wood and dressed and painted exactly as were the Katchinas. These were given to the children to teach them of these mysterious and wonderful beings.

After the crops had been harvested and the year was drawing towards winter, came the time of the nine-day ceremonies. All during the year rituals and dances were held,

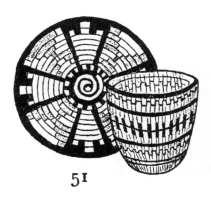

51

but the spring and summer were busy months and the rituals could not then be so long. When the ceremonial dances were held the villages were alive with movement and color. The deep-toned drums and the insistent gourd rattles sharply emphasized the cadenced chants as the pageantry of prayer was enacted by the people. Before the altars and shrines were placed the prayer plumes of eagle feathers. When the sun came up in a yellow line over the horizon, it would see the prayer plumes and carry their message onward. Eagle feathers were a necessary part of every ceremony. Young eaglets were caught and raised in captivity so that feathers were on hand when wanted.

The most sacred and mysterious ceremonial of all was the Snake Dance. From the four directions of the desert the reptiles were gathered and carried through the figures of the dance. Then they were released to bear the prayers for rain to the underworld from whence came the first human beings. A snake moved with the darting swiftness of lightning; its tongue was forked as a lightning flash. A snake moved as the curving streams flowed across the desert. The snake was a powerful messenger, for it was seldom indeed that the rain failed to come after the dance.

One of the prettiest of the many ceremonials was the Butterfly Dance. It began when the sun was high in the heavens and lasted until it had left the sky. The young girls stepped sedately through the intricate movements, wearing high wooden tablets upon their heads and carrying bunches of green sprigs in their hands. The young men also took part in the dance for it was a dance of youth. It told of the little corn-maiden plants that would grow tall and strong with the falling rain.

Hopi men wore their hair in bangs across the forehead, cut square below the ears, with the long back hair tied in a bundle at the neck. Unmarried maidens dressed their hair in whorls at each side of the head that were meant to look like squash blossoms. When they were married the hair was worn in two coils which hung down over the shoulders.

Because the Hopi did so much running, many of their games were running and racing ones, for in this way they further developed endurance and swiftness of foot. In one game, two small painted sticks, or a stone ball, were kicked in a race in a large circuit around the fields. This was not only carried on for sport, but was also supposed to

protect the fields from the harmful sandstorms through some magic power. Hopi children liked to walk on stilts.

Today the Hopi live in their mesa-top villages much as they did when they were found by the Spaniards. Of all the beautiful baskets made in the region, theirs are the most highly colored. Each of the various Pueblos has a distinctive type of pottery that is easily recognized and Hopi ware ranks among the finest. In color it is light cream and blends through orange and red. They are content and at peace in their remote dwelling places just as they have been for centuries—for Hopi means "peaceful."

PEOPLE OF THE WANDERING FLOCKS
(The Navajo)

The Fierce Ones had swept down from the north. They had driven the First People up into the cliffs, and remained to wander the desert and to prey upon the weak. They did not want to plant crops, for they were hunters of game. They did not want to stay in one place for they were wayward and restless. They did not know how to make pottery or basketry and they were not desirous of such things that belonged to a settled civilization. It was an easy matter to descend suddenly from out of nowhere and seize the corn of the desert dwellers when it was ripe and ready for gathering. Bowls and baskets if needed could be obtained in trade or stolen as well.

The Navajo is descended from these early raiders, and he always remained a wanderer. Let those who would do the work of pottery making or basket weaving. The Navajo preferred to roam free and unhampered.

The Spanish explorers brought sheep and horses with them, and it was not long before some of these fell into the hands of the desert looters. In a very short time they became a nation of horsemen and shepherds. They still moved about, but they moved with their sheep from pasture to pasture. Lawless ways were no longer followed for the Navajo had become peaceful and industrious.

So these followers of the flocks traversed the wide reaches of this arid land. Their log and earth covered hogans were built wherever the family paused that the sheep

might graze. Close beside the hut of logs stood the loom that was such an important part of Navajo life. From the sheep came wool that was brown, black, white, and gray. From the desert plants came dyes for coloring. The natural wools and those that were dyed were woven into blankets of surpassing beauty and durability.

It is believed that the art of weaving was learned from the Pueblo Indians whose women were captured in the early forays. But legends say that the craft was taught by the Spider Woman when the world was very new. At any rate, the Navajo, who was rarely the creator, but always the borrower and improver of the creations of others, became famous for his woven blankets which rank among the finest of primitive weavings. Among the Hopi the man did most of such work but it was the Navajo woman who was the artist of the loom.

Spider Woman taught many things to the Navajo. She even taught them how to play a game of weaving designs with string upon the fingers. White children play this game and call it "Cat's-cradle." But there were many more and different designs in the Indian playing. Fingers had to be expert indeed to manipulate the string into the intricate patterns.

From the Spaniard and the Mexican the Navajo learned the art of silver work, and here again he became the master craftsman, excelling those who were his teachers. The primitive anvil, the crude tools for etching and hammering, were as important to the man as the loom was to the woman. From silver coins he fashioned rings and bracelets, saddle and bridle decorations, bow-guards, beads and pendants, in seemingly a thousand variations. The azure blue of the turquoise insets added the final touch of beauty. All the tribes of the region eagerly bartered for Navajo silver and turquoise ornaments.

Like his Pueblo neighbors, the Navajo had many ceremonies. But where the Pueblo danced, the Navajo sang, and dancing had only a small place in his ceremonials. Where the Pueblo rites were essentially prayers for rain, the Navajo were for the healing of the sick. The most powerful healing rite was the sand painting, which was begun at sunrise and destroyed at sundown. The gods were the first makers of the paintings and they drew them upon the black clouds. But the people living on the earth could not draw upon clouds and they did not have the magic materials with which the gods could paint.

Then, said the gods, take the colored rocks and minerals of the desert, grind them into fine powder and make the picture upon the golden sand. Thus it was that the one who had the right to carry out this sacred duty spread the clean sand upon the floor of the medicine hogan. From his bark trays of color, a small quantity of the holy powder was taken between the thumb and first and second fingers. As his hand moved over the base of sand, the powder trickled forth to make the painting. There was no line so fine, or detail so complex that it could not be drawn, and a large painting meant hours of patient labor. The forms of the gods, of the lightning, the clouds and the rainbow, and of objects having a religious meaning were the subjects of the drawings. They could be made only in the winter time, and so from winter to winter they remained locked in the minds of those who drew them. Yet they never faded from the memory, and from generation to generation each painting was always the same.

In the ceremony of healing, the person to be cured was placed within the center of the completed picture, and the chanting and the rituals began. Any person within the hogan who was ill could take a small portion of the sacred painting and share in its wonder-working power. When the ceremony was done, powdered rock and golden sand were taken back to the desert from whence they came.

The Navajo is still the nomad, wandering from pasture to pasture and watching over his flocks of sheep. Descendants of a stranger race that came into the southwest to plunder and destroy, they remained to become a very part of the country. In his ceremonials, the Navajo chants that he "walks in beauty, with beauty above him, and around him, and below him." He sees this beauty everywhere in the land that he made his own. Today the Navajo are the largest tribe of Indians in the United States.

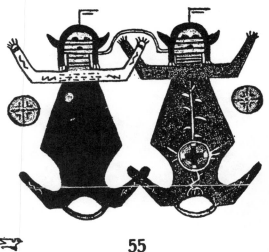

WHERE WERE
THE DWELLERS ALONG THE SEA COAST?

Starting at the Oregon-Washington border and running northward to Alaska.

Some Principal Tribes of the Region	Where They Lived	Where They Are Now
BELLA COOLA	British Columbia	British Columbia
DUWAMISH	Washington	Washington
HAIDA	Queen Charlotte Islands	Queen Charlotte Islands, Alaska
KWAKIUTL	British Columbia	British Columbia
MAKAH	Washington	Washington
NISQUALLI	Washington	Washington
NOOTKA	Vancouver Island	Vancouver Island
PUYALLUP	Washington	Washington
SALISH	British Columbia	British Columbia
SNOHOMISH	Washington	Washington
SWINOMISH	Washington	Washington
TLINKIT	Southeastern Alaska	Canada, Alaska
TSIMSHIAN	British Columbia	British Columbia

CHAPTER SIX
Dwellers Along the Sea Coast

ON the north Pacific shore stood forests of giant spruce and cedar. The sea thundered upon the coast that was rugged and deeply carved with bays and inlets from the pounding of the waves. Down from the inland slopes swift running rivers made their way to the ocean that was never still. Clustered along the beach and shadowed by the huge trees were the plank house villages of the northwest Indian.

The interior country was rough and barren. The forests were so deep and dense that people could not live within them. These trees did not bear fruits or nuts for food, and so thickly did they grow, and of such great size, that the forest could not be cleared for gardens. But the sea lay at the very doors of the Northwest People and the sea became their world. Fearlessly they went forth upon the restless waves to harpoon the whale that with one blow of its mighty tail could break their largest craft to pieces. Up and down the coast they traveled, to trade or to attack other villages and carry off the captured ones for slaves. Their dipping paddles moved in rhythm to chanted songs that had the steady yet broken beat of the wave-drums of the ocean.

A canoe of bark was too frail to stand the lashing waters. Boats for sea travel must be large and strong. They were made from a cedar log several feet in diameter. A fallen log was preferred and one that was covered with moss, for this generally contained the best wood. Before a log was selected, a small hole was cut in it to see if the heart wood was sound. The boat was the most important possession of these sea-faring people and their lives depended on whether it was well made, of good, solid wood.

The building of a canoe required many weeks of hard work, for the log must be hollowed out so that it was long and tapering. From a hard greenish stone called "jade-

ite," the Indian carver made tools that were harder than flint, and with a cutting edge that remained sharp for a long time. With such tools even these huge logs could be chipped; fire helped in the hollowing out. Canoes might be small enough to hold only two persons, or large enough to hold fifty.

When a log for a canoe was shaped and ready it was necessary to spread the side walls and to form the prow so that the edges would keep out the rolling waves. The boat was filled with cold water into which heated stones were dropped. When it was steaming hot it yielded to the hewn plank wedges that were forced into the hollowed out space and slowly pried the walls apart. The edges turned over and outward and prevented the waves from dashing inside. The prow was wonderfully carved with faces and figures of bear or otter, forms of birds, or creatures of the sea. These faces gave to the canoe the same qualities of strength or swiftness or ability in the water that belonged to the living things which they represented.

With so much easily worked wood about, the Northwest Indians naturally developed into master carvers and builders. They knew nothing of machinery, and had only their stone implements and wedges of wood or bone. They did not even have the simple pulley. Yet they could cut down the monster trees of the country and shape them as they wished, and they solved the problems connected with moving such large timber. The logs were dragged down to the sea and towed to the village. Skids were used for rolling logs into place for building or for the convenience of the carver or workman. Poles were erected by placing the butt end in a pit dug with one sloping side and were then raised upright by pushing and pulling with ropes made of twisted cedar branches or thongs of rawhide. To place a roof-beam into position they levered it up a sloping log whose end rested on top of a supporting pillar.

The houses were fashioned from planks split out of the great cedars, smoothed by long and patient labor, and were often over 75 feet long and 20 feet wide. House planks came from standing trees, or from logs that were split into the desired thicknesses by means of wedges. If a standing tree was used it was one that had been dead at least two years so that it was well seasoned. There were always some of these standing-dead trees ready for service. Living trees were first selected and then girdled by chipping away the bark close to the roots all around the tree. It was left in the forest while its life was slowly destroyed and after the proper length of drying and seasoning time it could be cut when needed. The planks could be split out of the standing tree.

Squared wooden boxes, steamed and carefully bent and then joined with spruce root fibres, took the place of the pottery, basketry, and rawhide containers of other tribes. Wooden helmets that were carved likenesses of birds or animals were worn in warfare, and carved masks in ceremonial dances. Many of these masks were astonishing, indeed. Some of them were faces within faces. A string pulled open the first face and there was another of entirely different character. Some had beaks that opened and closed, eyes and eyebrows and lips that moved, and other movable features.

The north coast Indian knew nothing of the buffalo and he did not raise any crops. The rivers ran thick with salmon and within the sea were halibut, seals and whales. Though the people ate of the flesh of bear, deer, and moose, yet it was on the salmon that they depended the year around. Wild berries grew in great quantities and these provided them with vegetable food.

From cedar fibres and roots of spruce, beautiful and finely textured baskets were made. Wide, peaked hats of basketry were worn to protect the head for this was a rainy country. The simple clothing that was worn was woven from the long hair of the mountain sheep and shredded cedar bark. Blankets in soft shades of blues, yellows, greens, and blacks were made of this hair and bark material and traded throughout the region. In cold weather robes and clothes of skin and fur were used.

Designs on carvings, paintings or weavings were perhaps the strangest and most striking of any in aboriginal America. Every part of an object must be covered—there must be no blank spaces and all parts of that which was to be pictured must be shown. An animal design could be cut into bits and scattered about like a jigsaw puzzle. It made no difference as long as the form was there in its entirety. The tail of an animal might be above its head, and the wings of a bird placed beside its legs. Tucked in corners and bare places were circles for eyes, rounded rectangles for joints, and other strange and complicated symbols. Sometimes a creature was shown as though split in two and then flattened out in two joined profiles.

59

One who did not know could never guess what the picture was intended to be. But the Indians knew by ears placed over the head that it was of an animal, or that it was a person if the ears were found at the side. Large incisor teeth and a scaly tail were shown for a beaver. A straight beak identified the raven and a curved beak the eagle. A long tongue was part of the grizzly bear.

Copper was looked upon as the possession of greatest worth. Copper was found in lumps or sheets in formations of rock, or where it may have been deposited by ice or water carrying it away from its original location. It was pounded and shaped into knives or arrow points. It was made into tools or fashioned into bracelets. The man who owned much copper was very rich. In the homes of the wealthy, thin copper shields, called "coppers," were hung upon the walls. They were shaped something like an axe blade. They were in size from a foot to three feet across, and decorated with the weird designs that were characteristic of these people. These hanging shields were the tokens of the importance and position of a family.

Almost as valuable as the "coppers" were the planks from which the houses were built, for these planks had been obtained at the cost of a great deal of hard and long labor. When it became necessary to move a house or to build a new one, it was carefully taken apart and the planks used over again. The building of a house called for the work of a number of men, sometimes of a whole community. The completion of a house was always a time for festivity and rejoicing that a difficult task had been accomplished.

PEOPLE OF THE TOTEM POLES
(The Kwakiutl)

From out of a mysterious and wonderful beginning a family might be founded. In the story of its years there were heroes deserving of honor, or powerful spirits that had helped and befriended. What better way to preserve such stories so others could know of the family greatness than to carve them upon the trees? A carved tree could stand for all who saw to read. Wind and rain would not harm it; the carvings would not wear away. A tree was majestic, beautiful and worthy to tell the history of the people.

60

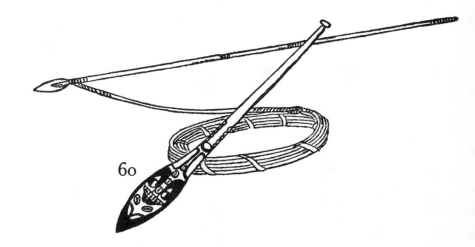

Before the houses stood these carved tree posts, or totem poles, that sometimes rose to a height of fifty or sixty feet. Strange figures were cut upon them to tell of family ancestors or family happenings. Grinning or scowling faces, whales and fish, men with spears, bears and ravens, and the Bird of the Storms with outstretched wings. The story was begun at the top and read down from a distant and mystic past to the figure of the owner of the pole that stood at the base. Totem comes from the word "ototeman" which can be translated as "his brother-sister kin." With its many totem poles, a Northwest village bristled like the back of a porcupine with upright quills.

The Kwakiutl say that they did not always have totem poles. They did not have them until the chieftain, Wakiash, brought one back from a world above the sky.

To the Kwakiutl, blankets, coppers, totem poles, all had their worth, but a name was more valuable than any of these. When a boy-child was born, it was named for its birthplace. Within the year a new name was purchased by the parents. The articles of purchase were carved dishes of the black slate that was found in the region, woven mats, and paddles heavy with carving.

Later on, when the boy had reached the age of ten or twelve, a third name was bought, and this time blankets were the purchasing price. But for every blanket given away, a blanket must be returned before the year was up. Five blankets given, meant that ten came back to the giver. As quickly as they were received they were distributed again, so that blankets were constantly in circulation earning interest for the youth who would some day grow up to possess a fortune in credit. It might happen that the necessary hundred per cent repayment on a gift could not be made. Then a man could place his name in pawn for a year and during that time it could not be used or spoken. A pawned name had to be redeemed at even a higher rate of interest.

These blanket "gifts," or loans, were presented with great ceremony at the feast called the potlatch. The Kwakiutl dearly loved to possess property, because they also loved to give it away at the potlatch feast and in this way display their wealth to the world. But though a man might beggar himself in providing food and presents for all, in the end he was even richer than before for his credit was exactly double what it had been.

A leader of note, when giving a potlatch, would provide the finest of foods, and most bountifully. There would be quantities of fresh or dried salmon. There would be cakes made of pounded and dried berries, and such roots and seeds as were good to eat. There would be the meat of seal, or whale, or bear, and thick pieces of halibut. Dishes of warm grease, or the oil from fish, were provided to dip the food into for added flavor.

Specially invited to the feast would be the head of a rival family, and custom demanded that the invitation be accepted. Blankets were heaped before this rival. Gifts of skins, of articles of household use, and sometimes even the cedar canoes. In turn, the honored guest must equal gift for gift. If he was given one hundred blankets, he must place one hundred blankets upon the pile, and then all two hundred were his property. But later on he must return, at another feast, four hundred blankets, or his family would suffer loss of rank.

Most dreaded of all potlatch gifts were the copper shields that hung upon the house walls. The original value of one of these shields was not more than a few blankets. But with every potlatch the value of a shield increased one hundred per cent, and it soon reached a fabulous figure. Some coppers have been known to be worth six thousand blankets. The ceremonial value of those that have been handed down for many generations can only be guessed at. Coppers, too, had names that told of the dread in which they were held.

Sometimes a man was able to acquire enough wealth to pay for a copper shield in full. If he wished to show that so valuable a possession meant little to him and thus boast of his superior position, he would break it into pieces and cast it into the sea. Such a deed brought everlasting fame. He could preserve it in song, in story, and in carving, for now he was a man above others.

Perhaps a man could not possibly repay all his potlatch gifts with their one hundred per cent interest. Such misfortune brought deepest disgrace. The one to whom he was in debt could then sing sarcastic songs about him, or carve a humiliating and mocking wooden likeness to be set up where all could see and know of his shame. So overwhelming was this disgrace that he might cast himself into the sea like one of the broken coppers.

If a feast giver found that he did not have enough presents to make the proper showing, he could borrow from relative and family connections, but every such borrowing had to be repaid. Men of importance were hopelessly in debt, and these debts were passed from one generation to another for years to come. Little children could recite the family debts just as children of today can recite the multiplication tables. Kwakiutl children grew up with the responsibility of paying on these debts to maintain the family position, and a family that did not have such obligations was lacking in honor.

Truly a man's name was his fortune. Among other tribes a name might speak of such brave deeds that an enemy heart would be stirred with fear. It could be a "joke name," or a "clan name," or a name of spiritual significance. But only in this land of the north did a name have the power to purchase.